Melbourne Cup Day

Our Favourite Race Day

Dear Mum and Dad,

Dear Mum and Dad,

We went to the races.

Dear Mum and Dad,

We went to the races.

We looked at the horses.

Dear Mum and Dad,

We went to the races.

We looked at the horses.

I had a ride on a pony.

Dear Mum and Dad,

We went to the races.

We looked at the horses.

I had a ride on a pony.

I had my face painted.

Dear Mum and Dad,

We went to the races.

We looked at the horses.

I had a ride on a pony.

I had my face painted.

We looked at the hats.

I liked the red hat. Nana

liked the orange hat.

Dear Mum and Dad,

We went to the races.

We looked at the horses.

I had a ride on a pony.

I had my face painted.

We looked at the hats.

I liked the red hat. Nana liked the orange hat.

We saw the race!

The horses ran very fast.

Dear Mum and Dad,

We went to the races.

We looked at the horses.

I had a ride on a pony.

I had my face painted.

We looked at the hats.

I liked the red hat. Nana

liked the orange hat.

We saw the race!

The horses ran very fast.

Dear Mum and Dad,

We went to the races.

We looked at the horses.

I had a ride on a pony.

I had my face painted.

We looked at the hats.

I liked the red hat. Nana liked the orange hat.

We saw the race!

The horses ran very fast.

Melbourne Cup Day is a special day

Love from Sally.